VARIABLE DUSK

23
/100

David J. Martin

David J Martin
Visit the author at www.duskbook.co.uk

Printed in the United Kingdom

First Printing: March 2009

ISBN - 978-0-9561520-0-8

David J Martin

Variable Dusk

CONTENTS

Introduction

Welcome to *Variable Dusk:* a collection of poems by me, David J
Martin. Yes, the J really does make me sound important, doesn't it?

Ah, poetry. What is it…?

Well, with metaphor this, iambic pentameter that and well, other
bewildering poetic terms and devices… it's obviously an art that
requires a lot of patience and thought! But does poetry *really* have to be
crammed so full of things that most people would never notice anyway?

I think not! What (I think) it *does* have to be is a collection of words
that can evoke a range of thoughts and emotions. Simple! And isn't that
special in itself? Simply looking at ink spattered about on the page and
finding yourself *feeling* something because of that? It's the reason I
started writing in the first place and it's bloody magical! I wrote
Variable Dusk with this view in mind.

So, whether the following pieces are what you would call poems,
doggerels or ditties; whether you would call me a poet, versifier or
something I dare not repeat! I hope you ENJOY what I present to you
now. I wrote these for YOU and you alone, because YOU are *special.*
Thank you.

Acknowledgements

This book would not have been possible without the influence of the following people, so thank you:

My wonderful parents, Ged and Jacqui; for all of your love, commitment, and sacrifices you made to give me the best childhood I could have asked for. For staying together. For moulding me into a good person. Most of all, for giving me the opportunity to *live.* I love you both.

My beautiful partner, Danielle; for always taking time to listen, and, often, for giving me the first great (but definitely not biased!) opinion of my work. For supporting me through it all and helping me to remain focused on what matters. I love you.

Cup of Tea

I would like you to take a minute now,
As you drink your cup of tea,
To consider all of the things involved
That have been, to make it be.

Consider the man who founded the tree.
Consider the slaves and their pain.
Consider the ships that sailed, and then
Consider the cows and the rain.

We can apply all of this to most things.
All we have and all we see,
Has been shaped by the past, be it happy or sad…
Not forgetting, *you and me.*

So now, as your mind paints a picture,
What there do you see?
Do you see a tale spanning years and years,
Or do you see… a cup of tea?

Drink up.

Burn Me & Bury Me

If you'd ask me how I'd like to die,
I'd say I'd like to drown,
So I'm cleansed of the effluence of Earth,
When I'm dipping down.

But when I'm dead, please burn me,
And turn me into granite;
Then bury me to keep me
From the people of this planet.

Yes, *burn me and bury me*
And wipe from Earth my name,
So I'm not amongst those reckless thugs,
The dying World will blame.

A Tree

A tree has helped the vast skies form
The darkest dusk and the brightest dawn,
A tree has nourished the life of Earth,
A tree has sheltered timorous birth.

A tree has forgiven the strongest gale,
The coldest rain and the hardest hail,
A tree has gave all it has to give,
A tree has helped us all to live.

Muhjubruga

"Muhjubruga Fuhjubree!"
That's what the alien said to me.
"Fuhjubruga Muhjubree!"
That's what his little one said to me.
"Jubree Jubruga, Muh Fuh Jubree!"
That's what his old man said to me.

And I'll always remember what they said to me
For all had their very own way.
But I regret to think, that on that very day...
I had nothing to say.

Opposites

Declaring I'm right declares you are wrong,
I beg to differ; *you agree.*
Differing is our speciality.

You love to hate [me], I hate to love [you]
They say that opposites attract!
… Like a KNIFE to a sack.

The Unsure Guest

An alien passed by our World,
One starry, mystic night
And pondered at the sphere of life…
Then faded out of sight.

He might have stayed to greet us, he
May well have brought a friend
But to land on Earth and meet us (he thought)
Would surely mean his end.

His tears fell down two hundred miles
And landed in the sea,
As he considered all the dry brown land,
Neglected by the green.

He said, "these people are abominable!
'We come in peace' they'll say!
But they slaughter all of their OWN creatures,
And murder *every* day!

These skies are blackened with terrible filth!
These waters polluted with dirt!
The animals, utterly helpless I see
And innocent folk are hurt!"

So off he went. But where? Unknown.
And *never* shall we know.
And he'll probably never return to meet us,
Though you may see his U.F.O…

A Grandmother's Pain

A Grandmother makes you feel at home.
Her heart is gold, her touch is warm.
She welcomes you with total love…
A smile, a kiss… *an oven glove!*

She'll not be pleased until you're full,
And when you are, *she'll offer more!*

But when you leave; the smile (by tears),
Is washed away, and leaves her fears,
Of falling, or having a *heart attack…*
The kind, old lady shivers and cracks,
Form on her tired, grey face.

Days may pass with no-one to see,
(Except for the salesman, with fake I.D)
A Grandmother cries when all alone,
Her character dies in the silent home.

But what was that? You're here again!
The smile breaks free! (Disguising pain).
It's been some days since you've cared to show,
But it's fine…she looks glad! So it's time to go.

…You bastards.

The Same

People aren't so dissimilar
We're born and then we die, you see.
In between, we're quite familiar,
Or at least, we're forced to try to be.

The Star

At night, I look to see the Star,
I hope you see it too.
I know it shines on where you are...
The Star is my link to you.

I love to look towards the sky
And think of what's below.
I don't mean seas, or mountains high,
But you, you're there, I know.

I love to drive on scenic ways
And think of where to go.
I don't do it to find the days,
But you, you're there, I know.

I love to sit for quiet rests
And watch the people flow:
A river passing through my quest,
For you, you're there, I know.

And if my time should come to die
My last breath, pure and true,
Will blow a kiss towards the sky...
The Star is my link to you.

Sweeping Hands

There once was a man who lived his days
Many years have since perished.
His name has since been naturally erased,
Like all those he loved and cherished.

Tick tock, and the hands of the clock...
They have swept the names away.

I'm now a man, and I live my days,
In a World where few know my name.
In years to come, I'll be fully erased,
With only *myself* to blame.

Tick tock, and the hands of the clock...
They will NOT sweep my name away.

The Centre

I am at the centre of the Universe.
You are at the centre too.
For the Universe spans as far from me
As it spans as far from you!

A Dismal Connection

The baby shits in his nappy,
The old man shits in his pad.
The baby is crazily happy,
The old man is fucking mad.

The baby wears a bib for feeding,
The old man wears an apron.
The baby cries to explain his needing,
The old man weeps for attention.

The old man shall weep, and the baby will cry,
But one has a life, and the other shall *die.*

When the baby does not understand,
It's fine, for it will do soon.
The old man who can't, on the other hand,
Is an incomprehensible loon.

Oh woe, for the way we grow,
To become the same thing as before.
There is one depressing difference though:
We're not welcomed, but *kicked* through the door.

The Jam Covered Mongoose

When I die, I won't go to heaven, for heaven does not exist.
I'm sorry to all you Christians, but *please* don't be pissed.

When I die, I'll not be back, reincarnation's just as mad.
I'm sorry to all who thought you'd return, but *please* don't be sad.

When I die, there'll be no soul, for the body *and* mind will die.
I'm sorry to all who thought you'd live on, but there is no need to cry!

Because there exists a giant mongoose that swims in a river of jam.
When we die, we'll appear on its back and hold onto a string of ham.
The other deceased shall discuss our journey towards the magical light,
As the mongoose breaks wind and the jam splashes up, we will feel as high as a kite!

Now what makes me laugh is the notion I speak of is just as feasible as yours!
And you will never be able to otherwise say until you depart through 'the doors'.
You may laugh, like me, at my idea, but would you care to prove me wrong?
In fact, SHUT UP for just a minute, while I break into a song!

"I am the Almighty Mongoose that swimeth in a river of jam.
As I paddle towards the magical light, hold onto your string of ham.
Oi!"

The Tastiest Pie

The crooked man, he baked a pie,
Mixed in a big brown bowl.
Into the mix, he whisked a fly,
And sprinkled the hair of a mole!

He cracked an egg and poured some rye,
"A bit of it all!" he'd shout.
"Nobody can bake a better pie!"
As he threw in the head of a trout!

The oven was opened; the steaming pie,
I admit, did smell quite nice.
But had to think of the baked blue fly,
As he offered to me a slice!

The man was saddened by my decline
And offered some to the crowd.
The people cried out 'just divine!'
As through the pie they ploughed!

And to this day, I still hear them say,
It was the TASTIEST pie in the world!
But I know the pie was far from gourmet,
As into the mix, a fly was swirled!

A Smile

A smile presented to somebody sad,
May make them a little more happy.
A smile presented to somebody mad,
May make them a little less snappy!

A smile presented to someone reserved,
May make them a little more easy.
A smile presented to someone unnerved,
May make them a little less queasy!

Such a simple and wonderful thing: a smile,
A vision unlike any other.
It can make this life seem more worthwhile;
Disguising a lot of the bother!

The Lady Too Late

He wasn't well, so he'd stay in his chair,
But she was worse and she couldn't bear
His orders, every *single* day,
Her chances of *life* slipping swiftly away.

She was old and frail with a heart of gold,
But it weighed her down; she would not be told
To *leave him*, not to leave it too late,
But she'd serve up her health on a china plate.

When he left the room for a little while,
She would tell me how she'd forgot how to smile.
The room with him felt like a morgue,
So silent, so dead… he would never talk,

Except for to give her more chores to do,
She was all he had, he was all she knew.
There was never a thank you; all that he blew,
Was surrounded by smoke, though her breathing he knew

Was not very good (that man was *obscene*),
Her lungs were abating; she needed machines.
But physical health was the last on her mind,
It was sanity, the thought... could she leave him behind?

Eventually, she decided she *had* to go.
It would kill her to stay with him and so,
She walked right out and smiled inside,
But just one week later… the lady died.

THE Generation

In the future, there will be happiness
In *everyone* you see.
Friends more, enemies less,
And *everybody* free.

And it'll all be thanks to a team
Of one moment in existence
That took a stand for a dream
With pride and persistence.

Wouldn't it be truly great?
To have been *THE* generation?
To have quashed the racial hate
Of *every* single nation?

Regarded as we're gods and more
By the future population;
Those grateful for our peaceful war
Against racial discrimination?

And yes, it really can take place!
We don't have to walk a mile…
Just shake hands with another race
And share with them a smile.

Now & Then

Now is now, and then was then,
And now becomes then, now and then.
But if now 'becomes' then, then then must be NOW.
I confuse myself, now and then!

Variable Dusk

The clouds waft smoky dew along an awesome golden ray
That penetrates my soul and bonds this one enchanting day
To my memories of existence, and yet, *I search for more,*
Vivacious colours dance above the darkening Earth floor.

I drive in my car; en route, I speed, for the puddle *it* goes under.
I open my window and rowdily scream... my muddles gently sunder.
The twilight air blasts in my face; I breathe it deep inside.
I feel so peculiar in this place, at the phase where beauty hides.

The sky has strokes of blue behind a flickering of grey,
Scarlet wisps entwined about a thicker *ringed* array.
Of orange, whites and yellows joined, descending to the ground,
I journey alone, but long to share this beauty I have found.

Though tomorrow, a new dusk comes; the patterns I see now drown.
They'll soon be gone forever... the sun is going down.

I Will Not Weep

If I never see men of all colours join hands,
Or animals equal in ruling the lands,
If war on this Earth is never to cease,
I will not weep. I will not weep.

If I'm never to walk with the giants of Earth
Or behold a new life through the wonder of birth,
If over the pit of my fears, I can't leap,
I will not weep. I will not weep.

If I'm never to find my soul-mate, my wife,
If I never discover my meaning in life,
If dreams I hold dear, I'm never to reap,
I will not weep. I will not weep.

The views I have, I will always keep,
And to this world, I will never weep,
For one day soon, I shall go to sleep
And it will happen for me in heaven.

Dear Stranger

I have yet to even meet you,
But I always know you're there.
Each day your face comes into view,
To remind me *life's not fair.*

I think of you when good food I eat,
But more when my plate holds waste.
When the child is ill of too many a sweet,
A thing you have never to taste.

I think of you when I am warm in my bed,
But more when I'm cooled by the rain.
When people see storms as a thing of dread
As your family endure dry pain.

I think of you when relations are home,
But more when I say goodbye,
When people fight hard just to be alone,
While you watch your family die.

I look to the sky and I hope and pray
For the world to be equal and free.
And I question each and every day
Why you are in Africa instead of me.

For now, I wish you know I see,
It's not enough just to look up above.
There is a reason why you visit me…
And one day soon, you will feel my love.

Bottle of Destruction

Today an extraordinary thing occurred.
I was sitting by the mere;
The water was still, not shaken nor stirred,
When a bottle did appear!

It started bobbing up and down,
Plastic, small and empty.
It had a label, but I saw that drown,
(Until the advertisers pay me).

All of a sudden, I heard a voice.
It told me loud and clear,
To sink the bottle! I had no choice!
The end of the universe was near!

So, I picked up a rock and threw it,
And it splashed in the water nearby…
The bottle shook, but I knew it
Was going to take another try!

So I tried and tried, but missed again.
I began to feel quite scared…
The voice was echoing in my brain,
"Nothing will be spared!"

I stopped a moment to ponder the facts
And consider the voices' demands.
To this threat, I had to react!
The fate of creation was in my hands!

But the bottle was not sinking!
And the time was drawing near!
So, I ran to the edge without thinking
And I dived into the mere!

I splashed and splashed but was shocked to find,
The bottle… it was not there!

I thought I was losing my sodden mind
As I noticed the people stare.

So I pulled myself back up on the bank
And the bottle appeared once more!
But in minutes, the thing had fully sank
And the water was still like before.

The Note I Carried

Dear family, officers, coroner, too,
I welcome you to look at my face;
My eyes are closed, I do not move,
But I smile in *another* place…

You'll know I saved a life today
In quite a selfless act.
If not, please throw this note away,
But allow me to explain 'the pact'.

I'd never liked the idea of dying,
Not least an undignified death,
Being remembered as a man crying
As he choked on his final breath.

No, I wished to go out a *hero,*
So I pray that's how it's ended.
I promised myself I could let go,
Of life… while a life I defended.

Perhaps I saved a child from a blaze
Or rescued a pup from a storm?
Sheltered a man from giant waves
Or stood between him and a gun?

Whatever it was, I am now at peace
And I wish for my family to see
My love for you shall never cease.
My heart on Earth will forever be.

So please don't cry for me, just know
That before I left, I smiled,
To be regarded in life as a hero
And live on in the eyes of a child.

An Educated Letter

The clouds are low tonight,
Thick and silver, they layer the sky
And mystical streaks of light
Fall from the moon and fuse with the tide.

The faint cry of the gull,
Is my sole reminder, life is still here.
Though the moon is big and full,
I envisage its light through a solitary tear.

This is an educated letter,
Not a mere selection of spite-riddled scrawl.
I am wise enough to know better…
I may have gone, but it's you who will fall.

I walk upon the sand,
The markings we made have long washed away.
The winds replace your hand,
As the sea, your heart, so cold and grey.

There was beauty on this beach.
I would never have guessed so much could occur,
But it all seems out of reach
When my arms are folded to stop my heart from EXPLODING from my
CHEST!!!!

'THIS!!' is spite-riddled scrawl, you CHEATING BITCH!!!!

I HOPE YOU CAN EXPLAIN TO MY FAMILY WHY I AM DEAD.

My Fondest Dream

Tonight I will enter a magical land,
Where the natural world is glad,
Where black and white go hand in hand,
And it's impossible to be sad!

Tonight I will sail through a wholesome mist,
And soar off into space.
I will raze a comet with a prodigious fist,
And save the human race.

Tonight I'll become a most famous artist,
With exceptionally brilliant skills.
I'll be the greatest human to ever exist,
And make cancer-killing pills.

On second thought, as nice as they are,
These dreams just will not do…
So instead I will gaze at the lustrous stars
And simply think of you!

Seduction

Answers
Beyond
Corrective
Deliberation

Endlessly
Formulate
Gnawing
Hesitation

Ingenious
Jibes
Knowingly
Linger

Mindfully
Nearing
Openly
Pulling her

Questioning
Reality
Set in a
Trance

Unaware
Vafrous
Whispers of
Xenomancy

Yield
Zygnomic charms…

He Strides Over Stars

He strides over stars,
His eyes are alight
with the flames He will raise
when He reaches the world
that He made with His hands
and He can't understand
why respects were not paid to its beauty.

The wondrous skies of a
prospering world
full of natural joy
held alluring aromas of flowers and trees
that we've masked with the smog and pollution
of death,
and things we don't need.

What gives us the right to abuse it?
We're tenants on Earth,
we should live by the landowner's rules
but we take it for granted
and soon we shall see
that our lack of respect
has been noted.

An infinite pain in His heart
like the mother who has to
choose death over life
when she trembles and places her hand
on the switch
to turn off the machine
giving hope;
giving *air* to her child.

He cries in despair
and wiping the tears from His smouldering gaze,
fire comes again:
the anger He feels in His soul is as hot as

the millions of stars
He destroys in His rage.

One simple task that He gave
was to love,
to share and to care for our brothers on Earth.
Instead we live lives full of greed and disgust;
we were given a chance
but dismissed it from hand.

He knows of the Saints
and the good people here
but this cancer on Earth
has begun to spread faster
than ever before,
leading people to war,
even those who are pure being forced to forget.

We lose our control,
blasting holes in the face of creation,
His makings,
destroying this world...
Choose wishes of men over His?
He won't tolerate this
from the life He created with trust.

And virus of evil
remains in the lives
of select human beings
as the eyes of a puppy
repeat in His mind,
through every stride,
when she's tied to a tree
by the man that she trusts:

She playfully wags
for such love she had found
in a species that others would hide from,
but then she was scared

because this stuff was cold
and it smelt rather strong
then she squeals,
As he burns her alive.

And cries of a baby
just 12 weeks on Earth
being laid on a bed by her father,
who silently closes the door
and with no one to see
puts a hand on her mouth;
she's unable to scream.

He strides over stars
and shaking His head,
He roars at an army of angels
gathered before Him;
forgiveness they plead, but
like rocks of erupting volcanoes
they're smashed with a blistering fist.

In fury He'll strike
and the oceans and seas will turn red
with the blood of us all
and evaporate up
to the sinuous crimson and black,
causing blood to rain down on our memories corpse.

We 'are' His creation but so is the Earth,
He created it first and for this
He will not let it die
so protect it He shall,
in removing the tumour His hands
will make final our fate.

The sickness of Earth shall be cured
and again it shall live life of
pure, utter bliss
for the good will ascend,

it will rise from the evil below,
He will turn and go forth to the Heavens.

He strides over stars,
His eyes are alight
with the flames He will raise
when He reaches the world
that He made with His hands
and He can't understand
why respects were not paid to its beauty.

But Never Bush

The mighty Earth revolves;
it fluently evolves…
It feels not the explosions,
but resolves ghastly erosions
being brought about by men
and lightens day, again…

And when it turns to darken night,
the Earth, I trust with all its might
to make our precious day return;
to let light in, but never burn.
To bring the dark, but never freeze,
to journey smooth; not tip the seas.
To show us beauty, let us see,
to simply live and let us be…

I gave the mighty Earth my trust;
my trust I'll *never* give to Bush.
But, for my willful words of worth,
to take my trust, *he'll take the Earth…*

The mighty moon appears
and gradually, it nears…
It shines upon the stricken,
and the tears of soldiers glisten
as it soars across the night
Dissolving into light…

And when it journeys back to sight,
the moon, I trust with all its might
to grace us with its silver flare,
to circle close, to soar with care.
To dodge the path where sunlight flows,
to raise romance, to tint the rose,
to give us hope, to pull the tides,
to light the place where beauty hides…

I gave the mighty moon my trust;
my trust I'll *never* give to Bush.
And since I'll never trust this loon
to take my trust, *he'll take the moon...*

The mighty heart pulsates
through ever-changing states.
It yields not to the madness,
but creates a home for sadness,
and it beats on evermore...
Through all the pain of war.

And when it nears its greatest plight,
my heart I trust with all it's might,
to carry on with strength and will,
to not give in, to not take ill.
To welcome love, accept it true,
to fear not death; to red the blue.
To uphold peace and love in all,
to give to others, aid their call.
To be as one with Earth, and then
accept as equals... all Her men...

I gave the mighty heart my trust,
my trust I'll *never* give to Bush.
He'll take the Earth and Moon to start,
But *NEVER shall he take my heart...*

The Leaves of Autumn

The leaves of autumn touched her dress as gently as they fell,
And vivid crimson light caressed the hair I loved to smell.
Her delicate hands I held on to, as I looked her in the eye,
She smiled and said: "I love you… I'll never say goodbye".

With golden light upon her face, and stars within her eyes,
My fingers tenderly touched to trace reflections of the skies.
She closed her eyes and heaved a sigh, collapsing in my arms,
And winds so gentle passed on by to steal her scented charms.

I held her tight and ran my fingers firmly through her hair,
I breathed her sweet perfume that lingered faintly in the air.
She looked at me with earnest eyes and lips beseeching mine,
A gaze to make my deep soul rise, and darkness in me, shine.

I pulled her in and kissed her lips, with passion burning wild.
Stroking past her slender hips, she curled a naughty smile.
On a bed of vibrant autumn leaves, I lay her down to rest,
And kissed her silky neck so soft and licked down to her chest.

I peeled her dress, on hips it hung, her perfect breasts exposed.
I flicked her nipples with my tongue then playfully with my nose.
She smiled so sweetly, tilted high and pushed my head below,
I licked and kissed around her thighs, while stroking nice and slow.

I pushed the skirt up past her waist, her panties to the side,
And savoured her delicious taste with moist and tender glides.
She quivered, gave a blissful moan; I forced my tongue in deep,
In harmony with grateful groans, I let her juices seep.

Inviting me, her legs spread wide, I joined her graceful dance,
I pushed myself so deep inside, her eyes rolled back in trance.
We writhed in rhythmic ecstasy, as birds sang Twilight's tune
And night wolves howled mysteriously towards the rising moon.

Now sat alone, amongst the trees, I'm longing for her touch,
I feel her warmth still on the leaves, the golden leaves I clutch.

In anguish, I must face the skies as tears roll down my face...
And autumn leaves fall, laced with lies, land softly in her place.

Such Is Life

Such is life when waters flow
To thwart the sun and drown your glow.
A grain of sand beneath the shore,
You're bounded by a billion more.

Such is life when mountains rise
To lift you up to lonely skies.
A blade of grass below the frost,
Your colour slain and litheness lost.

Such is life when zephyrs touch
To ease you from the bough you clutch.
A falling leaf amidst the trees,
You're taken swift with frightful ease.

Such is life when all you gain
Dissolves around your faded name.
A drop of rain, you fall so free,
To merge, forgotten, with the sea.

Know Me Not

My love, I die now, before your eyes,
But please, I wish you know
That love transcends our physical lives,
So here, now, before I go...

Please know me not by sight, you see
I am not there... that is not me.
I am not matter illumed by light;
I exist in the dark of the night.

Know me not by sound, you see
I am not there... that is not me.
I am not words directed by tone;
I exist when you hang up the phone.

Know me not by smell, you see
I am not there... that is not me.
I am not notes of a chemical scent;
I exist when the bottle is spent.

Know me not by sense at all,
For darkened nights and muted calls,
And spent cologne, will soon arrive...
And even though: I'm still alive.

Know me not by taste, you see
I am not there... that is not me.
I am not flavour your lips touch upon;
I exist when the kisses have gone.

Know me not by touch, you see
I am not there... that is not me.
I am not felt with the trace of a hand;
I exist when our bodies disband.

I am always there, like I always was,
I wish you to know this now, because,

You'll sense me not; but you're never to fear,
For within your heart... I am always near.

You're A Star

You ever sensed a loving wish?
Or felt
Admiring gazes
from afar?
At times you feel alone
remember
who you are…

Life is full of magic,
but these
questions unrequited
are still here…
The very essence
of your truth
is blighted:

…must be more…

There 'is' much more to life,
and though
at times, you'll feel dejected,
hope won't die…
Pathetic demons
have your mind
infected:

…this I'm sure…

Know *you're worth much more!*
'Cause while
the skies go on forever
you should know
you're at the centre,
of it all:
It spans from you.

The Universe is 'yours',

it's true!
Perception is the answer
to your pain…
Imagination is the
key you need
to gain.

The rising moon may shine
so bright
and laugh towards the tiny
light afar…
(aware not of its might)
you'll always be
that star…

The star that shines upon
our lives
a vital a sense of *warmth*
is what you give…
I pray, you *must* be strong
you mustn't fade
but live.

The strength you hold within your heart,
will let
you glow forever.
All around
the empty space is dark:
but *you're* forever found.

You ever sensed a loving wish?
Or felt
Admiring gazes
from afar?
At times you feel alone
remember
who you are…

The Dismal Truth (To Kill A World)

At birth
we start to breathe
a vital need…
for oxygen
our bodies feed
upon, until
it's gone
we turn it into
poison…

To CO_2
and then we do
the same as
power plants
we breathe it out,
into the air
we cannot care…
we *need* to breathe.

And soon
we start to feed
a vital need…
to eat the food
of Mother Earth.
We strip it bare,
we cannot care…
we *need* to feed.

To feed upon
the creatures who
we have to kill
to have our fill,
and then
we shit them out at will
we shit them on the Earth.

The seas

we load
with waste
the case
should not be what
but *why*
and though we try
to clean our mess,
the fact remains
until we die…

We *have* to live.
We *have* to feed.
The history
of life
that spans
millennia
agrees…
we're born with *needs,*
that state a purpose:
To *survive.*

We build the things
we do not need,
for someone thought
that brains were marked
by aptitude
of using tools…
technology hacks the way...

Through trees
The very source
of life
removed
depleting what
was rife.
Our needs
concealed by
needless greed
desires

that have no ground.

Our factories
destroy with ease
and even still,
they help us stay alive,
but will the Earth survive?
We loot it of its *fuel*...

To satisfy
temptation
of the Nations
greed succeeds
and urges men
to kill:
a need
that has been programmed
in our lives.

A virus
is created
to destroy:
to KILL.
Commanding what is good,
it carries on
for if it stops
it will expire.

We *must* respire.
We *must* consume.
And reproduce
until our doom...

And it *will* come,
BEFORE you get your 'reason'.
Such a shame
that in the seconds
we have left
we'll learn 'the *purpose*,

was to blame'…

FORGET
'the vows of love you make.'
FORGET
the 'word of God'.
FORGET
'your fate'
'your soul-mate'
views 'to make
the Earth
a better place'…
FORGET
it all…
it's why we're here,
and even though we try…
the only way we'll ever save this Earth,
is if we
DIE.

Just A Drink

The night was young
and so was she.
Just seventeen,
with eyes of icy blue,
her smile as white as glue
would fix you to her gaze.

The emerald rays
and silver strobes
would dance upon
her shiny raven hair;
her scent controlled the air…
and spellbound, *they* would near.

The men would leer
And offer gifts,
all types and size.
Attentive to her class,
they'd fill the finest glass
with colours wild, as she.

She moved so free
she twirled just like
a flower on
an airy autumn eve,
but when she went to leave
she wilted, fresh, no more.

And through the door
she stumbled with
a stranger whom,
relinquished all his charms,
to have her in his arms…
(he'd gave her just a drink).

Then on the brink
of consciousness

she peeled away
the dress upon her skin
to let his *games* begin,
and drifted into clouds…

Now, wrapped in shrouds,
her beauty lies...
she's raped and just
a shadow of the girl
who brightened up the world…
and all for *just a drink.*

The Word I Heard

The age of two
I heard the word.
The word I heard
Was *love*, you see
And it may be
I heard the word
To one day share
With you.

When I was three
I said the word.
The word I heard,
I *said*, you see
And it may be
I heard the word
To say one day
To you.

The age of four
I wrote the word.
The word I heard,
I *wrote*, you see
And it may be
I heard the word,
To one day write
To you.

When I was five
I sang the word.
The word I heard,
I *sang*, you see
And it may be,
I heard the word,
To sing one day
To you.

The years gone by

I used the word.
The word I heard,
I *used*, you see
Improperly…
I used the word.
I'll 'feel' one day
For you.

And when I die
I'll know the word.
The word I heard,
I'll *know*, you see
Was you with me.
And with the word,
I'll say goodbye
To you.

The Lonesome Mr. Lightwind

The Lonesome Mr. Lightwind had no face.
A feature for description? Not a trace.
Not a nose, an ear, a mouth nor an eye...
He was plainer than a cloud in the sky.

He wondered *why* he had no face,
Yet still could see, and smell, and taste,
And hear, and even speak out loud,
But tired he was of resembling a cloud.

He wasn't proud but to and fro,
To public places, he would go.
He'd stare at people, give a sigh,
"How are you...?" (They passed him by).

"I wonder why my life is such,
That I should hate myself so much.
That I should cry but shed no tear,
That I must live... this lonely year."

So it was here, he made the choice,
To paint his face and raise his voice.
And so he drifted through the place,
Where birds would fly and dogs would chase.

He built a face with leaves and grass,
But people turned to let him pass.
He wept... this life just wasn't fair,
He wondered why they didn't care.

"As if I'm air, you look through me!
How rude can all you people be??
Trust, I see what I find in you...
Be kind enough to see me too!"

Now this was new (they turned to gape).
Alas, it was a bit too late.

For Mr. Lightwind changed his face,
He'd lost his faith within our race.

"An empty space! You see me?? NO!!"
And so he ranted to and fro.
He howled and whirred to make his mark,
Then suddenly… the skies went dark.

And through the park, the people ran,
But Mr. Lightwind had a plan...
He caught a tree within his sight
And toppled it with all his might.

And like a kite, the branches soared,
Then crashed upon the parkland floor.
People bawled; they shrieked with fear
As Mr. Lightwind *shed a tear…*

He said: *"Oh dear, what have I done?*
Why have I made those people run?"
Then let his sudden fury wane
And washed away his face with rain.

He felt ashamed and though he tried
To forget… our Mr. Lightwind cried…
The sodden leaves upon the floor,
Confirming *there was nothing more.*

And oh so sure now on that day,
They'd never again come look his way,
He swiftly scaled a tree to grieve,
And took his life, *with falling leaves.*

Shut Your Mouth!

At times in life, in times of strife,
I feel distressed, and in my quest,
To feel at ease, I ask you please...
To shut your FUCKING MOUTH!

I can't believe that shit can leave
Your ugly face... I feel disgraced.
Your plastic breath will cause my death...
So shut your FUCKING MOUTH!

It's hard enough to deal with stuff,
Without your crap; I swear I'll snap
Your jaw in two. (I've snapped a few!)
So shut your FUCKING MOUTH!

Oh please dear God...! You noisy sod!
You're driving me, INSANE you see...!
I'll burst your lung! Remove your tongue!
So shut your FUCKING MOUTH!

You make no SENSE! And so intense,
Your words go on, but please, BE GONE!
I cannot stand you, 'understand' you?
Shut your FUCKING MOUTH!

You make me CRY! So now you'll DIE!
Smashed by hammer, now you stammer!
GOUGE YOUR EYES! It's no surprise...
I HATE YOU...

FUCKING FURBY!!!!

Awakened Muse

An empty page before me,
And try as though I might,
My Muse is cold and lonely.
I'm damned if I can write.

But there to help me progress,
I close my eyes to find....
The portrait of a princess,
Engraved upon my mind...

Her hair is long and soft and blonde,
My Muse, it will entice...
For of her hair, my Muse is fond,
it senses paradise...

And so, come thoughts of golden sands,
The freshness of the breeze...
Cracked coconuts within my hands,
And waves upon the seas...

I write through eyes of birds in flight,
Migrating from the cold...
The cool blue skies touch golden light,
The warmth they will behold.

But as I write the final line
And sign my name to close,
The wonders of my Muse recline,
Then back, behind, it goes...

Again, a page before me,
And try as though I might,
My Muse is cold and lonely.
I'm damned if I can write.

But there to help me progress,
I close my eyes to find....

The portrait of a princess,
Engraved upon my mind...

Her eyes, divine, they shine with care,
My Muse, they will allure...
And for her eyes, my Muse will share
A verse of love so pure.

And so, come thoughts of cobalt nights,
A star that glistens clear...
A red rose draped with silver lights
A single, joyful tear.

I write through eyes of utter bliss,
A romance warms within.
I dream of leaning close to kiss
Her gorgeous, velvet skin.

But as I write the final line
And sign my name to close,
The wonders of my Muse recline,
Then back, behind, it goes...

But even though it hides at times,
My Muse will never cease...
For beauty charms the dormant rhymes,
My thoughts of you release.

The Case of the Melted Emu

One day, an old man had a fall,
He'd blundered over *grease,*
Dead-centre of the Village Hall...
He dialled for the police.

His shaking fingers made the call,
A voice asked what was wrong.
"An Emu, melted! In the Hall!
So come, and don't be long!"

His screams attracted people who
Would gather when they could,
To solve the riddle, find the clue,
To make the village good.

A pool of feathered liquid formed
With beak and eyes intact,
Around it, all the people swarmed,
This case they wanted cracked.

"I've never seen a liquid-bird!
It's really rather strange!"
The voice belonged to Father Word,
The Vicar of the Grange.

"But surely, it's not 'that' bizarre!"
A mordant man remarked.
"The myth of 'God' tops this by far!"
Then one old lady barked:

"You vulgar teens, you're all the same!
You don't know when to shush!
I'd not be shocked if you're to blame,
For all this Emu slush!"

"Now just hang on," a lady said,
"We're not here for a row!

Is this poor Emu 'really' dead?
Will someone check him now?"

The people laughed and one man said,
"She's blonde, she's not to know!
There's not a brain cell in her head…
It was quite funny though!"

"What's funny? I think you're to blame!
The fact is that you're black!
I don't quite know from where you came,
But I think you should go back!"

"I don't agree with that!" One said,
"You see that man with braids?
Yes, HE'S the reason that bird's dead!
The gay man gave him AIDS!"

"Just hold it there," the old man said,
"We'll never solve this case
If all your puny minds are led
By stupid things like 'race'…

Inclined beliefs of creed and such,
And typecast views of gays,
And blondes, and youths, is it too much,
To quash your stubborn ways?"

The crowd was still: they pondered words
The old man said to them,
And looked down at the melted bird's,
Remains… (They looked like phlegm!)

"You're right! Your views are only fair!"
A woman shouted out.
"It's her… the girl that's got NO hair!
Watch out, the freak's about!"

The old man shrieked, "For goodness sake!"

(He almost, nearly swore!)
And then, he shook enough to make
A tube drop on the floor!

The people gasped to see this sight,
A boy said, "Was it YOU?
Did you melt that poor bird in spite?
Whatever did you do?"

The old man gasped and stumbled back,
"O.K, O.K!" he cried.
"The vial you see: I bought a pack…
It's Emu pesticide!

I really want you all to see,
That things can be explained,
A little bit more easily
If comradeship is gained.

And if you'd all just take the time
To quell your stupid flaws.
Instead of solving pointless crimes,
You'd open many doors!"

"You evil man!" a girl exclaimed.
Just then, the police came in…
They read the man his rights and, shamed,
The old man dipped his chin.

They jailed him up and locked the door,
He stands with ball and chain.
So reader, learn the moral or...
The Emu died in vain.

The Envious Obscene Lamb

Once there was a little lamb
With fleece as white as snow,
And everywhere that Chicken went,
The lamb was sure to go…

Our tale is set between the oaks,
Where creatures gathered round
One starry night, and told some jokes,
While one small creature frowned…

The pig had raised a simple view:
Just why did Chicken cross…?
He laughed out tales, then out the blue...
"YOU CREATURES MAKE 'ME' CROSS!"

"IT'S CHICKEN THIS AND CHICKEN THAT!
IT'S ALL I FUCKING HEAR!
HE CROSSED THE ROAD, THE STUPID TWAT!
AND ALL YOU BASTARDS CHEER!"

Right now, his eyes were bottle green,
His tongue was black as night...
"Good Lamb," said Pig, "please keep it clean!"
"WELL THAT'S A LOAD OF SHITE!"

"JUST WHY THE FUCK DID CHICKEN CROSS?
I GUESS WE'LL NEVER KNOW!
SO WHY SUCH FUSS? I'M AT A LOSS!
I'LL HAVE A TWATTING GO!"

The lamb barged out towards the road
And stamped his feet and baa'd.
Then suddenly, a heavy load
Come smashed his face in hard.

Alcoholic Foreplay

I walked in one night,
And there stood my wife.
She looked at me stern
While holding a knife!

"You have a nice drink?"
My wife scowled at me.
"I didn't", I said.
She added, "Let's see!

You've beer in your ear!
You've wine on your spine!
You've gin on your chin!"
"But honey, I'm fine!"

"YOU'VE WINE ON YOUR SPINE!
You've some on your tum!
You've scotch on your crotch!
You've rum on your bum!"

"I've rum on my bum?"
"Champagne on your brain!
You've dregs on your legs!"
"Good God, you're insane!"

*"To empty the bin,
That's why I went out!
And when I returned,
You started to shout!*

*I must say, in truth,
I find it quite odd!
Just put the knife down,
And look at YOUR bod!*

*You've schnapps on your baps!
You've drips on your nips!*

You've sangria here!
You've drips on your hips!

You've ale on your nail!
A bit on your clit!
A shot on your bot!
And bits on your tits!"

"How did you do that?"
She stammered to say.
To her, I replied,
"With alcohol play!"

"Of course, I recall!"
She slurred with much grace,
"We had so much fun!
So why the long face?"

I looked with a cringe,
And sipped on my beer,
Then turned to my wife,
And said simply: *"Dear...*

An Aftershock cock,
Is ok, my lass...
But why did you put...
The GLASS UP MY ASS?"

The Nose Knows

IN A LIFT
WAS A MAN
THERE WAS NOISE
THERE WAS SMELL
IN A LIFT
WAS A MAN
AND THE CAUSE
'HE' WOULD TELL…

The head said:
"The eyes lie
The ears fear
And this is why.
If you've a query,
Ask the nose…
The nose knows,
You see."

"Just go below
And ask the toe…"
The toe said "No!
I do not know!
Go ask the cheek,
And he shall speak.
The nose knows,
You see!"

The eye said "Aye, it's true I lie!"
The ear said "'Ere, I fear."
The cheek said "Cheek!
I will not speak.
Go ask the toe,
My dear!"

The toe said "NO!
I DO NOT KNOW!
Go ask the nose,

He knows!
So off you go,
IGNORE the toe...
The nose knows,
You see!"

The nose said "Oh!
It's true, I know!
From where that smell has came!
Sniffed to and fro,
And found that no,
The toe is NOT to blame!

And neither are the feet, its true!
The cheek: he would not speak!
For *he surrounds* the reason you,
And all these people seek!

The eyes? They lie, for they can't see it,
Ears? They fear the sound.
The cheeks? They can't, and won't admit it...
This is what I've found!

THE BUM... HAS... FARTED!"

The eyes were wise,
The ears, their fears,
Were proven by the nose.
And all the guys
Discerned their rears
And everybody froze.

Then those of whom
That had their nose
Alert them to the fart
Escaped the fumes
And on their toes
They swiftly did depart.

DON'T MESS WITH THE NOSE,
THE ALMIGHTY NOSE,
FOR THE NOSE KNOWS,
YOU SEE.

You're More

A black man looked at a white man.
"I am black", he said.
"This colour defines who I am,
From my toes, to the top of my head".

A white man looked at a black man.
"I am white", he said.
"This colour defines who I am,
From my toes, to the top of my head".

A gay man looked at a straight man.
"I am gay", he said.
"One factor defines who I am,
The person who lies in my bed".

A straight man looked at a gay man.
"I am straight", he said.
"One factor defines who I am,
The person who lies in my bed".

An old man looked at a young man.
"I am old", he said.
"My age is defining who I am,
And will do until I am dead".

A young man looked at an old man.
"I am young", he said.
"My age is defining who I am,
And will do until I am dead".

A writer inferred to his reader,
"I suggest," he said,
"You take not the stance that the people do
In the poem you've just read."

Personified Punctuation

!

The Exclamation Mark is blue today.
He QUESTIONS his EXISTENCE.
"Why, oh why, oh WHY", he says,
"Does calm fall in my absence?"

"MUST I FIRE the glad words up?
I feel like such a nuisance!
…am I really needed now?
Or am I just a HINDRANCE?"

.

The Full Stop's in a spot of bother.
 He QUESTIONS WHY he's here.
"Why, oh why, oh WHY", he says,
"Must the end come when I'm near?"

"MUST I END the glad words' fun?
I'm sure it's me they fear.
…am I really needed now?
Or should I DISAPPEAR?"

?

The Question Mark is reasoning,
He'd QUESTION his EXISTENCE,
Instead, he's busy questioning,
The life of EVERY instance.

"MUST the Exclamation moan…?
He bursts with bouncy brilliance!
MUST the Stop be feeling down?
His presence STARTS A SENTENCE!"

,

The comma feels indifferent now,
He DOESN'T SAY A WORD.
He merely bows his head to allow
The others to be heard.

The END!.?,

Away From Words

To get away from words is hard,
For everything we say is formed
With letters, everything we read,
It's words our eyes do see.

And every time we write a letter,
Every single thought is laced
With words, so whether thought or spoken,
Written down or heard...

It's words, it's words and words again!
However do we break from
Such a curse? To have a break from all these words?
To have a *holiday*?

A poet works with words day in,
Day out, so when he needs a rest,
What should he do? There's little much
To truly set him free!

But I've a plan for all to see!
A word to help us all: a *power* word.
But those who feel they know its meaning
Know that *words* have little worth!

The word is *love,* a word that, change
Its name, would be the same for it's
A *feeling. Words* are overused
But feelings need no wording...

Like feelings when you kiss the one
You love: you disappear from life, from *words,*
From all things, but this wondrous place.
Your soul is rising and

You never need to think to know.
You never need a cause for what

You see. There's never a need for words
For hearts to bond *invisibly.*

I say all this 'cause though my words
May take my time, I wish you know
That when I kiss you, I am true;
Away from words... I'm pure.

And in that wholesome place I go
Where all the meanings disappear,
It's only *you* I need to be with;
Only you... I truly love you

And want to live my life with you
Then *every* day shall be the same.
A break away from words, to let the sound
Of beating hearts be heard.

And most of all I'd like for this,
For each and every single day,
This poet with you in his arms...
Will have a holiday!

The Night It Rained A Brain

The thought I shall retain forever,
Such a dreadful bane will sever
All judicious thinking; NEVER
Will I be sane again.

Before, I'd watch the bird-brained Heather
Tell us of the mundane weather.
Afterwards, we'd all endeavour
To disregard the rain.

But on the day I won't forget,
The rain she forecast wasn't wet.
The rain she forecast didn't patter.
The rain she forecast...
WAS GREY MATTER!

'A brainstorm brews!' The forecast cried.
"Where temporal lobes and neurons galore,
Will swiftly descend! You MUST ensure,
That you're indoors till dogs have died!"

Till dogs have died? My poor, poor hound!
I fell in anguish, to the ground.
I could not let my dog be slain
By the deathly blow of a falling brain!

And so I raced towards the shed
In which my pup did snore,
My neighbour yelled, *"Mind out ahead!"*
"I know!" I cried, "They pour!"

But then I tripped upon a hose!
And heard a person talk,
Of myelinated axons! No!
So, up to him I walked...

"Please tell me friend!" I said to him,
"Where are these brains of which you speak?"
"No brains, my friend... the Saxons team!
'My Linn hated' them, this week!"

"But what about brains? They're just as bad!"
"Are you ok? You're acting mad!"
"I'm totally sane! The brains will rain!
And fill the drains while dogs are slain!

That's what the weather forecast said!
To stay indoors till dogs are dead!
We must abstain from feeling pain;
We must not deign, but disdain rain!

We must regain our own domain!
Immortal gain we shall attain!
We must complain! We must campaign!
Immortal gain we shall attain!"

"I see your problem now", he said...
Your 'aid' has fallen off your head!
For Heather said not 'dogs have died',
But stay indoors, till 'FOGS SUBSIDE!'

"Where temporal lobes and neurons galore?"
"Be careful the boats on Northern shore!"
"Of course!" I said, and gave a grin...
Then woke my dog and took him in.

The truth was that I had no aid,
My hearing was just fine, I'm afraid,
The warning came, but just too late,
And all that was left to do was wait.

And so that night, I sat with my dog
And by my window, watched the fog
Engulf the land, and then it came...
The landing of that awful brain.

The thought I shall retain forever,
Such a dreadful bane will sever
All judicious thinking. NEVER
Will I be sane again.

Lost Without Lorf

While walking in the woods one day,
A couple came to lose their way...
"You've got us lost!" the young man said,
"It wasn't me!" the young girl pled.

Just then, a strange and eerie sight
Appeared in a fantastic light...
A *Martian* stepped from out the trees,
It said "Hallo, Eeee come whiff peas!"

He had no peas but threw a rose
Towards their feet (the couple froze).
"Lorf wheel find a way!" he said,
"Find Lorf whiff-in, and you'll be led!"

The young girl kneeled to take the rose,
"Ok," she said, "Well, I suppose
We find this 'Lorf' and ask him how
We find our way... is that... a cow?"

"Give it here!" the young man said,
"I'll rip the petals from its head,
And use them all to mark the way,
Right back here, if we should stray

While to the woods, we venture forth,
To find the creature they call 'Lorf',
Present him with the flower's stalk,
As a gift from us, and THEN he'll talk!

And yes, that IS a cow, I think!"
The creature gave them both a wink.
Then to the Martian, did profess:
"Moooooooooooooooooooo... yes?"

"Yes," said the Martian, "leaf them 'ere!
They don't know woff Lorf is, I fear!"

Both said bye and set off North.
The couple stood and pondered 'Lorf'.

And to this day, the couple stand,
Astray within a darkened land...
But strangely, though *they* age, nearby,
The rose doesn't EVER wilt or die.

And so they stay with stubborn pride,
But if they both would just decide
To trade the rose for a gentle kiss,
They'd find their way and live in bliss.

With Them I'll Walk

There would have been days in Shakespeare's life
Where trouble and strife and such were close.
A pivotal dose would strike him hard
And fuel the angst of that great Bard.

There would have been days in the life of Seuss
Where 'what's the use?' would be his stance.
A perishing dance, his muse dog-tired
Would rest and wait to be inspired.

There will come days in my own life
Where trouble and strife and lifeless muse,
Arrange as my shoes. Then Shakespeare I'll stalk,
And Seuss I will follow, till with them, I walk.

The Fly That Contemplated LIFE

Late one most mysterious night
There appeared a most fantastic sight.
A splendid beam of moon-given light
Did fall through a fluttering blind.

And what should it find? But a *curious* fly
Standing relaxed on a mirror nearby.
The creature just gazed at himself asking *'why'*?
(This question had plagued his mind).

"I go for a stroll and I'm risking my life
When out on a flight I hear screams.
Just why must I always be hated?
Created was I to be murdered, it seems.
Just here to bring constant annoyance, they're sure,
But for them I do think that I'm here to do more.
My gift is decaying the waste that they live
To create... but they take me for granted,
And give me the stigma of being the dirtiest
Thing on this Earth, but I know just what
I am worth. If only the man in his bed
Would awake with the beautiful view to give love in his head,
I know that together we'd do great things,
From God, love was granted to all *Earthlings*."

Averting his eyes to the old man who slept,
He readied his hesitant wings and leapt
To the bed where he landed and silently crept,
Up the sheets on the old man's chest.

And giving his best and loudest call,
He jumped in the air and bounced off the wall.
He circled the face, yelling, "Love to all!
Forgive you, I do... with love!

With lots of love! Forgive you I do".
Then down to the old man's heart he flew

To give him a cuddle of peace so a new,
Fresh start could pave the way

To a brighter day. But as daylight came,
It brought a man, with much the same
Old views. He struck and felt no shame,
Never knowing what the fly did say.

Piggy Back

Animals do what animals must,
For animals love and animals lust...

"What's that little green frog doing, Dad?"
"Oh, never mind him my son!
He's having a game of leap frog!
Just having a bit of fun!"

"What's that big black pig doing, Dad?"
"Oh, never mind him my son!
He's giving his friend a piggy back!
Just having a bit of fun!"

"What's that big brown bear doing, Dad?"
"Oh, never mind him my son!
He's giving his friend a bear hug!
Just having a bit of fun!"

"Ok, I think I get it, Dad!
Is that doggy having fun,
'Cause his friend is doing a doggy dance?"
"No... he's fucking him up the bum!"

They Shit Too!

The posh are delusional, great as they *seem,*
They don't seem to realize they're living a dream.
They seem to forget that, whatever they do,
We normal folk know that they have to shit too!

They scoff and they taunt while abusing our class,
They think that the sun's shining out of their ass!
But I laugh right back, for the fact of it is,
As posh as they are... they still have to piss!

They still have to puke and they swallow their spit,
And 'dolelite' or duke... we ALL have to shit!
We all suffer times when our pants get too tight,
Then ooze up our cracks and get covered in shite!

I love it that I can be conscious of that,
When an arrogant, snub-nosed, ass-headed twat
So rudely insists upon raising his nose.
(But remind me he does, that they still get crows!)

They're still full of snot and they still get zits,
And noble or not, we ALL get the shits!
We all suffer times when we feel a bit queer,
Get stuck to the toilet and have diarrhoea!

"Oh rather, old chap!" Oh rather, *FUCK OFF!*
And take your worms with you, you itchy-ass toff!
"Disgraceful behaviour!" Indeed that is true...
But so, Sir, is wanking! And that you do, too!

They still stroke the sausage and still flick the bird.
And curbside or cottage, we ALL need a turd!
We all suffer times when it just won't come out,
And accent or not, we strain and we shout!

"You should be ashamed!" For what I enquire?
Reminding you all that you're human? Well, SIRE...

87

You are, and I've just two more stanzas, my king,
Pay careful attention, or else kiss my ring...

Your bottoms have winnits, your knob's full of cheese,
You've skid marks and piss stains, and get STDs.
You drool in your sleep and you fart in the bath,
As posh as you are, you feel Nature's wrath!

Your feet smell of Edam, you've lice in your hair,
You sweat and you stink and you breathe the same air!
See, money and power may make you *feel* smart,
But Nature, you dimwit, can't tell us apart!

A Beastly Misunderstanding

Today I was startled, 'cause out of the blue,
My friend chimed in, *"I need a word with you!*
You tell me the truth and you tell it me now!
How could you be sleeping with animals? *How?*

You *really* disgust me!" And with that, he went…
So there, I did ponder, 'what could he have meant?'
My girlfriend's not *that* bad…! So, was he confused?
Perhaps he just misconstrued words I had used.

Like saying my girlfriend's a fox, which she is!
My ex was a cow and the next was a bitch!
The next was a whale; her hole was so big!
And the girlfriend before her was simply a pig!

A right filthy beast, she resides on a farm
With all sorts of creatures… I *never* would harm!
While there, I'd ride horses, (I mounted enough!)
And was tossed by a donkey! Oh man, he was rough!

My weakness was having her bare in my bed…
While licking her beaver, she gave me good head!
Then fucking her pussy, no, make that her ass!
And sucking her great tits… oh what a great lass!

Awkward it was when she gave me the crabs!
They nipped at my penis; I had to have jabs.
I had to use cream, and take tablets and that,
And I never again stuck my dick in her twat…!

Oh my! *That's* the word for a fish *up the duff!*
(It's not just a name for a part-below-muff!)
No wonder my friend conjured thoughts in his head;
He was building assumptions with words I had said!

Like when I said eels are stunning… (Their shocks!!)
And my favourite farm creatures are chickens/cocks!
But I'm fond of *all* creatures… o.k.; *one's quite shit*…
I'm not fussed on camels, and that's 'cause they spit…!

I once milked a cow, and it made me all wet…
For I jerked it too much. (Do I look like a vet?)
I've searched through a field and it's hard to find moles,
But that won't deter me from probing their holes!

My new chick is tasty….. she fucks like a tiger!
There's nothing I like more than lyin' beside her!
She's quite a short bird, her ethnicity: white…
I've not fucked a black bird but one day, I might!

Good God, she's amazing! A right little minx,
In bed, 'animal' can describe her… methinks!
She shags like a rabbit and makes me quite spunky…..
But when she's away, well, I must spank the monkey!

My girlfriend has puppies; don't ask me their names,
But I call one 'the runt' and he spoils all my games…
Well, I'm quite fond of sport and I really can't see,
Why he fucks with my stuff, so in turn, he fucks me!

He chomped on the racket I use to play squash,
So I'd take it for walks in the hope that I'd quash
His new habit of constantly chewing my balls!
(For I do love a vigorous bat up the walls!)

So every each day, I would work on that runt,
And I soon found he'd bark if I walked in up front.
That canine…! He really was one of a kind…
So I'd always be sure I would take it from behind!

He would lead me on and at times, too fast,

And one time, a cute little bitch ran past…
His nose caught the scent of her and in he honed,
So I pulled him so hard that he moaned and groaned!

A little *too* hard, many folk may allege,
So I gave him a taste of my meat and two veg
To make up for my crime, and now, speaking of food,
I've just thought what else could be seen to be rude!

I work as a chef so I think that my mate
May have heard me speak words of the food that I plate.
I may have said things like 'that lamb is quite *hot!*'
Or I've stuffed that nice turkey… I've stuffed it a lot!

Or maybe I've mentioned I like to eat fish,
Or a moist, tender chicken is wonderfully swish.
I will bite on its breast I will nibble its thigh,
And I'll yank off its meat… for its taste, I could die!

I will chew on its bone and I might even suck it,
When done, I will place it in my greasy bucket!
And after, I do like to finger a mousse!
Then savour it, spooning it, followed by juice!

I will put my thick sausage in the toad, in the hole,
And I like to roast poultry on my long, hot pole!
(Or spit as you call it). I do pork as well,
Pull the meat out the oven, and ring on my bell!

The fish that I smoke, well, I lure them myself,
With a vessel of seamen, I silently stealth.
And I aim my big rod at the waters below,
Put my bait in it's mouth, get a sackful and go!

Case solved! Yes, I think that my friend was misled,
For it seems there's more meanings to words I have said.

It's easy to see how my words are construed
To be something that's shocking and terribly rude!

I wonder how long he's been thinking that way,
And believing so strong to confront me today…
So, I best now go tell him I'm not a sick creep,
But first, I'll remove *my dick from this sheep!*

The Majority Has Switched

I used to possess a very good friend
And years we shared, but that was then.
I know all things must come to an end,
But, I just don't know *when*...

Could this just be another short break?
A parting, such to strengthen a bond?
Or has that passed, and should I awake
To the truth: *we both have moved on.*

It once was the case that my life, split in two
In the most would be blessed with their presence.
But now it is such, that the most part is due
To turn into the time of their absence.

I tried to believe that it hasn't been long
It's better for me, but reality *itched;*
The exactness of time cannot be wrong,
And the majority has switched...

I used to possess a very good friend
And years we shared, but that was then.
I know all things must come to an end,
But, I just don't know *when*...

I Became The Same

A woman I knew once confided in me;
She was fed up that men were just after one thing.
They would knowingly play on her naivety.
She hoped to have more than a fling.

Of course, I was different; of armies of men,
It was *me* that would listen and *me* that would care.
She demanded assurance, and every time when
She was down, I would always be there.

How stupid was I not to realise that she,
Who was asking for what I had put on display,
Had decided to call off her search prematurely.
Her sights were now pointed my way.

Then one fateful night, after drink, little tipsy,
As naïve as she, I succumbed to her cry
And I gave not a thought to the fact, with our lips,
To our bond, we were saying goodbye.

For days after that, when the question of what
It had meant did arise, as I tried to explain,
I should never have used the word 'fun', I should not.
It was then... *I became the same.*

A woman I knew once confided in me;
She was fed up that men were just after one thing.
They would knowingly play on her naivety.
She hoped to have more than a fling.

The CHICKEN on my Head

Late one night, I wrote berserkly;
Perky for my work was quirky,
Slightly smirky... jerky!
As I lay down and I read...

But in the murky darkness lurked 'he',
CHICKEN, as I read.

Lighting set to see my writing,
Righting wrongs I'd wrote, reciting.
THEN a sighting left me biting
Nails until I bled...

Fear igniting bird delighting
Cruelly, as I bled.

"CHICKEN, with your spiteful staring,
Glaring is that beak you're wearing!
Damn, you're daring! Sat preparing
Darkness in your head!

Foulness flaring; subtly sharing
Darkness, from your head".

- 'Surely dreams will halt despairing...
I shall rest my head'. -

Then he turned, that CHICKEN dancing,
Prancing, up my bed advancing...
Grimly glancing... *dancing!*
Was that CHICKEN on my bed...

Timely trancing, sheet romancing
CHICKEN, on my bed!

"No!" It seemed he'd *spied* me peeking,
Freaking at my mattress creaking!

Slyly sneaking… seeking
Something?! CHICKEN, bird of dread…

Bed sheet beaking, EVIL reeking
CHICKEN, bird of dread!

- How I wished that bird was Peking.
Here is what I said: -

"YOU from murky darkness lurking,
Watching, as my work I read, yes
YOU the fear igniting bird delighting
Cruelly, as I bled, yes
YOU uncaring, MONSTER sharing
Darkness that's inside your head!
You timely trancing, sheet romancing
CHICKEN
GET FROM OFF MY BED!

You bed sheet beaking, EVIL reeking
CHICKEN,
SPITEFUL BIRD OF DREAD!"

The CHICKEN seemed to like me crying;
Lying there… and started FLYING!
Terrifying CHICKEN flying
Down towards my head!

HORRIFYING, sense defying
CHICKEN on my head!

- How I wished that bird was FRYING…
SPITEFUL BIRD OF DREAD! –

"GO, be gone and leave me snoozing!"
Oozing darkness, CHICKEN… *fusing?*
So CONFUSING! Saneness losing!
CHICKEN *in* my head?

Brain abusing, muse infusing
CHICKEN *in* my head!

Peck-peck-pecking,
Peck-peck-pecking.

Peck.
Peck.
Peck.

Paigan

Paigan,

If only your eyes had allowed you to witness their stares; had they lasted a mere moment longer, you might just have realised how wanted you were, and been tempted to stay for a while.

Your beautiful smile had the power to take our cares and destroy them. You made us that little bit stronger. It's true you were loved by the people around you, but also by people afar.

I wished on The Star and I asked for a cure for your pain: all the time, having no-one approach you (for fears of rejection, they just didn't know that rejection was that which *you* felt). And so, many nights I was knelt saying prayers in vain; you had made up your mind, for you had to. You *had* to escape the neglect of the world and the hurt that was deep in your heart.

And I played my part... I am facing that truth every day. For I never did tell you how deeply I cared; how insanely besotted with all that you were, I'd become. I'd have saved your life. And all of the strife you would bravely dismiss, I would say: "Paigan, tell me! A problem that's shared is a problem that's halved... Paigan please, will you take off your mask?"

If only I'd asked, I'd have realised that such is the world: we assume Beauty's bound to be taken, and give not a thought to the fact *loneliness* is a threat to the hearts of us all.

So here, I now fall. I fall at the place where a girl shouldn't lie... but promise you Paigan, I do: From now on, I'll try to give voice to the Beauty, while always remembering you.

Always...

SKOON-BAH

TRILLIONS of creatures have lived on this Earth,
But NEVER have words of *spectacular* worth
Like *these*, been revealed... the greatest by far!
'Well SLAPETH MY TOE and call me a SKOON-BAH!'

TRILLIONS of creatures! That IS what you heard!
Not ONE of those creatures has uttered that word.
Sheep have come close... but close enough...? *NO!*
That word is by ME! So *SLAPETH MY TOE!*

INGENIOUS! Yes...? I thought so myself.
I may not hold records like: 'World's smallest Elf',
Or 'sexiest earlobe', or other grand feats.
My writing compares not to Byron or Keats.

But am I to care? Good BROOM, I am NOT!
If Shakespeare was better, so Good Brooming WHAT?
Would SKOON-BAH, *(to Shakespeare's words I relate)*
By any other name, not be just as great?

Well, NO! It's a SKOON-BAH, and *that* it shall stay,
Reminding us all that we could, any day,
Be first in the UNIVERSE... first to in time
Give LIFE to a new word, but SKOON-BAH is mine!

For Foggies

DOO HE…???
I fink he do…
I doon't nooo.
Nooo I doon't.

But I doo fink,
He LLLove-fitt
…
Yesh Yoo doo!

Do he luff duh…
Peesh uv himm?

NO HEE DOON'T

He luff duh
CHICKEN!!

Yesh he doo.

Free Food

Cheshire, Leicester, Applewood,
Brie and Dorset Blue,
Edam, Stilton, Cheddar… please!
Oh, and Tewkesbury too!
Hatherton and Wensleydale,
(I've nibbled quite a few!)
I really do like cheese, but see…
I don't… like… *you!*

I do like cheese, be it hard or soft,
CHEESE… do *you* like cheese?
I like cheese, all types, its true,
But try as I might, ***I DON'T LIKE YOU!***

Cabernet Sauvignon,
Beaujolais Nouveau,
Zinfandel, Madeira… please!
Pinot Noir, Bordeaux,
Shiraz, Syrah, Burgundy
(I've sipped on quite a few!)
I really do like wine, but see…
I don't… like… *you!*

I do like wine, be it white or red,
WINE… do *you* like wine?
I like wine, all types its true,
But try as I might, ***I DON'T LIKE YOU!***

- And now I'm full. Goodbye. -

Our Planet's Best

I sometimes sit and I wonder why
We search for life *outside* of Earth
As people *here* are forced to die
In wars of little worth.

I cannot help but sense the phrase:
'We come in peace' (you know the one)
Shall go unsaid until the days
When *human* life is gone…

'*Intelligent* life is there', we say;
Their wisdom surpasses our own, may be.
My guess? It does. This proved the day
They came and decided to *flee.*

But if they came back, well, tell me how
We men can think it's *us* they'd seek
To learn from! Me…? I feel a COW
Would prove our brains were weak!

For cows eat grass that, again, will grow.
Their waste helps nourish the ground; they rest,
And again, they eat, make waste, and so
On…*COWS are our Planet's Best!*

Perhaps this is why, when aliens come,
They abduct the cows to learn their rules,
Then, punish (with anal probes up our bum)
Us humans for being such fools.

Feathers

DEATH is a word I dislike very much,
And MORGUE; so *unspeakably* vile!
Such words conjure feelings of *fear*, so
I'll alter them.
These words shall make a man *smile*.

Death will be *feathers*,
And morgue shall be *breeze*.
Oh feathers and zephyrs
Do please!

I shall not be frightened when *feathers* float in!
Oh no! I shall welcome that day!
My body shall rest in the *breeze*, as
My *soul* ascends…
Then, in the clouds I shall play!

I Cheese My Pigeon

Rip. Crumble. Throw. Scatter.
Soon, they swoop;
Then, *pitter-patter…*

Pigeons stride upon my garden.
Me? I hide.

"I beg your pardon,
Bird," I whisper (oh so softly),
"Should you discover that bread to be *awfully*
Dry, I invite you to stay if you please.
I would like very much like if you…
HAD SOME *CHEESE!"*

Then jump!
I *pounce!*
And I grab me a pigeon!
"Nice CHEESE!"
I announce
As I pinch off a smidgen,
And smother him well,
From his head to toe!
So he's *totally* cheesed!
But *WHY?*
Want to know?

Well, some folk
Like to believe in religion.
But me? I am partial
To CHEESING A PIGEON!

But don't worry…
Its NICE cheese!

He likey.

My Hurt Is Hers

All my life, I've wished for peace.
A break from my own mind, it will
Not cease... the past is too unkind,
And so I can't be free.

For simple hurts expand in time.
I shouldn't let them hide, for it's
A crime, committing suicide;
Those thoughts are part of me.

But this *is* love, so surely now,
It's different? I should *trust* in change!
Her vow to love me must, it *must*
Be truth! Oh, let it be!

For I, in fact, could not believe
That angels were designed to come
Deceive the heart *they're sent to mind!*
I guess I'll have to see.

All my life, I've wished for peace.
A break from my own mind, it will
Not cease... the past is too unkind,
And so I can't be free.

But neither then...
Can she.

Dreams on Toast

Baked beans again; on toast they sat,
Two table spoons, no less.
Steam rose to warm my cheeks. "Eat up
Now son… no waste; no mess."

My parents, pleased to watch me eat,
Stood by. Their *eyes* were sad…
"There's dreams in them baked beans," said Dad,
"So eat up quick. Good lad.

They're magic beans, warmed up with a wish!
Our *special* wish for you."
Well the beans would fill me up each day,
So I'd always leave a few…

And I always thought, 'When do *they* eat?
So one night, after tea,
I crept to the kitchen, and there they stood,
Oh no… it couldn't be…

They were eating the beans I had left as waste!
(It seemed they always had).
And they murmured the noise of a famished pair…
I really love my dad,

And my mum; such love, for the fact was *they,*
Who were wasting away by the day,
Would selflessly starve to ensure *I* had eaten…
It's why I am here today.

And now, there's steak with trimmings galore!
I've a life that's so sublime!
But you know; I will still indulge in their *dreams*
On toast… from time to time.

New Curtains

I'm going to make a change to the world.
I can't tell you *what,* 'cause I just don't know.
And I won't, 'til the day when I'm suddenly hurled
Through the curtains, to start the show.

But I *am* going to make a change, don't you know?
It's an absolute must, though I don't know *when.*
And I won't, 'til the day when I'm suddenly thrown
Through the curtains, *but even then...*

I can't guarantee that I'll know what to do!
So it's needless to say; to my fate, I am blind.
But I'll hope nonetheless that the curtains are new,
And I'll pray that the crowd be kind.

POP

POP is all it takes, you know,
For a person who's barely arrived,
To go.
And now, I just can't help but see
That POP may be all it will take
For me.

Tin of Dog Meat

Two homeless folk were crouching beside
The wall of a shop; a man and his wife...
And I realised that what they were doing, was one
Of the kindest of things I had seen in my life.

Two starving dogs were eagerly waiting
As slowly, the man, upon that cruel street,
Spilled out on the pavement the food of a feast:
The gravy dunked chunks of a tin of dog meat.

Then oh, how they ate! Desperation alive!
Those dogs ate as though they had *never* before,
And the couple stood proud... were they starving themselves?
Were they pouring the last of their wealth on the floor?

Whatever their tale, and wherever they'd been,
The truth in the sight I was seeing that day
Was amazing; that humans were putting LIFE first
Not themselves... we are equal, I say!

Two homeless folk were crouching beside
The wall of a shop; a man and his wife...
And I realised that what they were doing, was one
Of the kindest of things I had seen in my life.

Simply This

Isn't it just pitiable?
Racism today.
Racists are PATHETIC.
That's all I have to say.